Decoration on Pottery
Trudie Alfred

Kangaroo Press

Contents

Foreword 3
Introduction 4
Decorating principles 5
Equipment 5
Decorative methods 6
Colouring oxides 6
Oxides in oxidation & reduction 7
Decorating with rutile 8
Slip decoration 8
Where to place your design 9
Glossary of terms 10

Drawings
Bands 11
Circles 17
Squares 25
Animals 33
Free shapes 39
Sliptrailing 53
Japanese brush painting 59

Colour plates   . . . between pp24&25

Pottery, photography and drawings: Trudie Alfred

Acknowledgments
My thanks go to the College of Oriental Arts, PO Box 445, Double Bay 2028, Sydney, Australia, for making the section on brush marking available for this book; and to the Australia Council for the Arts for giving me a grant for maintenance and equipment for research into design details.
My appreciation to my friends: Gwenda who made copies of the draft of this book, Elizabeth and Carmen for redrawing some of the designs, and to the kind people who encouraged me in my task.

© Trudie Alfred 1980 and 1988

This edition first published in 1988 by Kangaroo Press Pty Ltd
3 Whitehall Road (P.O. Box 75) Kenthurst 2156
Printed in Hong Kong by by Colorcraft Ltd

ISBN 0 86417 216 8

Foreword

There has been a world wide resurgence of craft pottery, especially over the last 16 years. During this time pottery has received emphasis right throughout the educational system in Australia and also in the community with many people wanting to participate on all levels of expertise and commitment. Part of the pleasure of making pottery is the joy and satisfaction to be gained from decorating clay surfaces.

Trudie Alfred, a well known potter who has been teaching pottery over the last 24 years, has recognised in her students a desire to decorate. She has also seen the tentative way in which beginners approach the task. In this book she has set out some valuable guidelines for students, giving them a starting point from which to experiment and increase their confidence.

This book will be welcomed by teachers and the many students of pottery who want to try their hand at decorating but are not sure just where to begin.

Janet Mansfield
Editor of "Pottery in Australia"

This book is dedicated to all my students past, present and future.

Introduction

In to-day's busy world the search for, and understanding of, one's own place in nature, and the conscious expression of one's surroundings are things which only a few can do. A student of any age, setting out into the new adventure of pottery, has to be guided through the vast body of existing material created from the earliest times to the present day. Many beautifully illustrated books have been published, and it is to be hoped the student will avail himself of these.

This book does not attempt to survey the history of pottery or the techniques of manufacture, but to encourage the use of applied design. The average student has not had the opportunity to attend design classes, and when confronted with the task of decorating a simple pot, find inspiration sometimes slow to emerge.

If glazes and glaze applications are not understood, the student has a hard battle before him. To produce a worthwhile object from the beginning is easier with the guidance of a resourceful teacher. A well-made pot is enhanced by decoration.

If you have ever made a pot you will want to decorate it. Expertise comes with experience and the choice of design will depend on individual taste and the degree of complexity of the potter's mind. Proficiency in other arts or crafts gives greater awareness and helps to achieve a personal statement with greater ease. The love and knowledge of music and dance can be most helpful in the understanding and execution of a more fluid line. An adventurous spirit is a great asset — the "daring to discover" a chance to overcome the mediocre.

This book is written especially for beginners in pottery. The designs are intended to help those who find it difficult to think of suitable decoration. The variety of designs presented may also encourage the construction of new pot shapes and the promotion of harmony between the two elements.

Some decorating principles

UNITY

In every design we aim to achieve unity:
form — line — colour — texture
The use of many elements may not necessarily produce successful results. The more complex and rich the design, the greater the control and balance must be to avoid chaos and retain unity.

LINE

A straight line . . . modern restrained, clear, pure.
Lines that constantly change can become weak and confused in character.
A curved line takes dominance over straight lines.
A circle is the most harmonious shape.

RHYTHM

The shape of the pot is all-important.
Design is additional and visually important.
Rhythm between pot-shape and design must be achieved: it should grow out of the object, be part of it and not something tacked on.
There are hidden rhythms and lines in every pot. The potter should be aware of these.

BALANCE

This is the formal or informal weighing of design elements.
The potter makes use of accent on form. Hollows hold shadows, projections catch light. Alternation of light and dark creates movement.

MODERATION

It is better to under-decorate than to obscure the fluid line of the pot. Leave enough blank background space to give the effect of simplicity. The design may help to accent or strengthen the shape of the pot, but should be done with restraint.

There is never one single correct solution, but many equally valid interpretations of these elements.

LINE — Straight lines varying only in direction, either vertical, horizontal or diagonal: staccato variations between lines.

CURVE — Series of degrees of curves, in totality amounting to a complete circle.

List of suggested equipment

A BANDING WHEEL: approx. 20 cm in diameter.

JAPANESE BRUSHES: fine and thick, coming to a point, and broad brushes squared at the top.

CALIPERS: approx. 15 cm.

KNIFE: a small pointed knife, not serrated.

LIDDED JARS with different coloured lids for easy recognition of pigments.

LINO-CUTTING TOOLS

MODELLING TOOLS IN WOOD OR METAL

LEAD PENCIL

RULER

PESTLE AND MORTAR, approx 15 cm.

SKETCHBOOK OR DESIGNING PAPER

SCISSORS

SPONGE (sea-sponge)

SPRAY GUN

CLOTH TAPE MEASURE

SYRINGE

Decorative Methods

There are many ways of using the designs in this book and no doubt you will devise your own manner of applying them, but be advised — unless skilled, make several test pots which can be easily put into a test kiln and the result quickly seen. If the result is pleasing, repeat on the piece you care about.

Brush painting : A soft pointed brush (Japanese) is used for painting. This can be done at all stages, before and after the first firing or before and after glazing the ware.
See further details on Page 11.

Burnishing : With stones, bones or spoons. The parts to be burnished must be very smooth and the clay body leatherhard.

Combing : Hold a coarse comb against the side of a vase or bowl while the surface of the clay is still plastic and raise or lower the comb to form a desired pattern.

Cord paddle : A flat piece of wood with plain or knotted cord or string wound around it. The knots can be placed at interesting intervals. This is impressed into the leatherhard pot by beating.

Decorations from doodles : A doodle design is placed on paper, and traced on the clay surface. Different oxides can be painted on all design areas or only into traced lines.

Inlay or Mishima : After tooling thick contrasting clay slip is painted into the carved surface of small or thinlined decoration. Bigger surfaces can have coils of different clay colours pressed into the incised patterns. Both clay bodies must be soft otherwise different shrinkage will occur.

Paper resist : Newspaper or tissue paper is cut into a pattern and dampened to adhere to the pot or plate — slip can than be poured over or oxides brushed over the exposed areas. When dry the paper pattern is removed.

Press rolling : This is used mainly for slabwork or tiles. Any object is pressed into the soft clay with a rolling pin. String, coarse or patterned material can be used, thin branches, flowers, shells etc.

Raised desgin : Soft coils are added onto the soft to leatherhard claybody.

Sgraffito : Scratching, scraping or tooling through a layer of applied dried slip; or on leatherhard to dry claybody.

Most designs can be used in a sgraffito (incised) manner, but the incision must *not* be sharp otherwise the design will be unpleasantly rough on the edges and the glaze may not cover it.

Slip : Contrasting coloured slip can be poured, painted, sprayed or syringed onto the clay surface. The clay body must be leatherhard.

Sliptrailing : Slip is trailed in a decorative movement onto the object. On soft to leatherhard claybody.

Sponge printing : An ordinary sea sponge or piece of thick felt can be dipped into an underglaze solution and repetitive patterns pressed onto the clay or glazed surface.

Sprigging : The application of pressmoulded clay ornaments to the object, on soft to leatherhard claybody.

Transfer printing : Oxides with water, brushed on a sheet of thin paper which is turned over and pressed against the clay surface, before the oxide has dried. Another design can then be superimposed, as the transfered application may be dotted or webbed.

Tooling
Carving
Incising : With wire-wood-shells-rope-gumnuts-metal-linotools, etc. On soft to leatherhard body. Some parts can then be rubbed or painted with oxides.

Wax resist : Beeswax or paraffin wax mixed with turps or kerosine is heated, applied to the leatherhard to hard surface and stains or oxides painted or sprayed over the parts not covered by the wax. This can also be done on a bisqued body.

Wheel and roller stamp : A design is pressed or cut into a leatherhard clayroller. When firm it is bisque fired and rolled evenly over the soft clay surface.

Colouring Oxides

Pigments are metal oxides, the same substances which colour natural rocks. When used on ceramic pottery the firing will change the colour according to *high* or *low* firing — *reduction* or *oxidation*. If oxides are watered down and not used to full strength, variations of *colour strength* will be achieved. It is also advisable to mix the oxide with a small amount of the same glaze as is used on the pot.
If oxides are used to paint the design on, they can be applied on either the green ware (dry unfired body), or on top of the bisqued ware (once-fired). Decorations can be painted with oxide onto the unfired glaze.
Oxides are applied just by mixing with a little water to a consistency that is not too thick, and a trial brushmark will tell if it is too watery. If too thickly applied, the oxide may flake off, or render the claybody impervious and the glaze may crawl away from it, which may only be seen after firing.
A better way of using oxides is to make a composition of oxides and clay slip. The more clay is used, the lighter the colour. A white clay is used for lighter results, but terracotta clay can be used, keeping in mind that the iron in the terracotta clay will influence the colour result.
This will also apply if oxides are painted onto a terracotta pottery piece, whether leatherhard, biscuited or glazed, unless the glaze used is white.

Colouring Oxides

COLOUR	OXIDE	FORMULA	ATMOSPHERE	REMARKS
Dark blue Medium blue Light blue	cobalt oxide cobalt carbonate	CoO $CoCO_3$	either	Stable, will not burn out, can spread due to flow of glaze.
Dark green Medium green Light green	copper oxide copper carbonate	CuO $CuCO_3$	oxidising oxidising oxidising	May run due to flow of glaze. Good for painting onto greenware for stable results. Lacks high temp. stability.
Dark purple Medium purple Light purple	manganese dioxide	MnO_3	oxidising	May run due to flow of glaze. Mild in intensity as a colourant.
Copper red Deep copper red Red to black	copper oxide copper carbonate	CuO $CuCO_3$	reducing	Stable if used on opaque or matt glaze.
Pale grey green Dark olive	iron oxide	Fe_2O_3	reducing	I. Small proportion of iron. II. Med. consistency.
Dark brown Medium brown Tan	iron oxide manganese dioxide	Fe_2O_3 MnO_3	either	Stable, may run due to flow of glaze. Good for painting onto greenware for stable results. Iron compounds impart yellow, red, buff, brown or black, depending on glaze composition.
Turquoise	copper carbonate	$CuCO_3$	oxidising	In an alkaline glaze a green turquoise will result in a Soda glaze, a real turquoise. In any glaze an excess of copper will produce a crystalline black.
Grey blue	{ cobalt carbonate ½ % { plus iron oxide 2%	$CuCO_3$ Fe_2O_3	either	
Purple blue	{ cobalt carbonate ½ % { plus manganese dioxide 5%	$CuCO_3$ MnO_3	either	
Bright leaf Green	Chrome	Cr_2O_3	either	Strong stable colour. Base glaze must be free of zinc oxide. Can cause pink tints on glazes containing Tin oxide.

Painting with oxides or pigments

If oxides are used to paint the design on, it can be applied on green ware (dry unfired body). Mix a little powdered china or ball clay with it. The oxide will be less likely to run. If put on a bisque pot, it is likely to smudge, when glaze is applied. If put on top of the glaze mix pigment with a small amount of glaze (same as the pot) otherwise glaze may not bleed through and cause dry patches.

Commonly used oxides are:

Iron oxides red brown	Cobalt oxide	blue
Manganese oxide brown to purple	Copper oxide	green
Chrome oxide green		

Refer to page 7 for firing details

Prepared underglazes

Underglazes are more stable than oxides and can be used on pre-bisqued ware and bisqued ware. Not all underglaze colours are fired to high temperatures and firing details should be sought.

Cobalt Blues

Cobalt used without additives can be very harsh and unpleasant and the mixing of iron oxide and or manganese oxide gives a muted effect.
Two good recipes for a blue pigment are (proportion by weight):

I.		II.	
cobalt oxide	2	cobalt carbonate	2
manganese oxide	4	tin oxide	2
iron oxide	3	talc	1
redfiring clay	1	red firing clay	15
		china clay	2
		iron oxide	5

These oxides should be thoroughly mixed in a mortar (the finer and longer the grinding the better) and water added; allowed to settle and tested for colour strength.

All oxides mentioned give a wide variety of colour, which depends on the composition of the glaze, the thickness applied and the firing conditions.

Decorating with Rutile

Rutile is an impure oxide of titanium. It contains small amounts of iron and vanadium.

When applied on its own, rutile flour mixed with water to a creamy consistency is painted in a desired design on top of a glazed pot and fired. No third firing is needed. Rutile can create an interesting effect on a dark brown glaze as the design can result in a light orange colour. Rutile can also be mixed with other colours, e.g. cobalt, copper or iron, and used in the same manner. Only small amounts of oxides should be added.

If you want to apply a dark brown design to a pot which has already a light glaze, try the following:

Feldspar	34 parts by weight
Iron Oxide	33 parts by weight
Rutile flour	33 parts by weight

This is best used on a stoneware glaze.

Slips

The fluid made by mixing dry clay and water in about equal proportion is known as *slip* or *engobe*. A pot after having been allowed to dry to just leather hardness can be covered or decorated with slip, by pouring the inside first and letting the shine of the slip become matte and then covering the outside by dunking or pouring. For decorative purposes a syringe can be used and patterns made with it.
A slip adheres well when its contraction during both drying and firing is approximately that of the body of the pot. For this reason one often uses the same clay in liquid form as that of the pot and just adds oxides.
White clay slip is sometimes required on a dark pot, but shrinkage difficulties may occur. An all-purpose slip can then be used.

White slip (parts by weight)

70	ball clay
20	flint
10	feldspar

White slip on a bisqued body (parts by weight)

60	china clay
20	ball clay
20	feldspar

Blue slip (parts by weight)

60	china clay
20	ball clay
20	feldspar
1	cobalt carbonate

Green slip (parts by weight)

60	china clay
20	ball clay
20	feldspar
6	chrome oxide

Black slip (parts by weight)

86	terracotta powdered clay body
10	iron oxide
5	manganese dioxide
0.5	cobalt oxide

Red slip (parts by weight)

80	china clay
12	feldspar
8	flint
20	red iron oxide

Tan slip: same as above but reduce the iron to 5 parts

To prepare slip, first weigh the dry ingredients, then add to them enough water to make a creamy slip. To keep the slip in good suspension add to a litre of slip ¼ cup of epsom salts diluted in boiling water. Stir the slip well and screen through an 80-mesh sieve. The consistency of slip is controlled by the amount of water used in mixing the batch. It is advisable to have 2 buckets of slip, one thin and one thick, depending on the method of decoration.

Where to place your design

You are a beginner potter and you would like to choose a design that appeals. You have the choice of many decorating principles detailed in this book. Read through the decorating ideas and find one that you would like. For instance: painting with an oxide. This can be done as soon as the pot is leatherhard. If you are not sure where it is best to place the decoration these pointers may help.

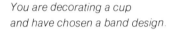

You are decorating a cup and have chosen a band design.

It is best to place the design in the middle or just a little higher towards the rim. If using a motive, place it either opposite the handle or on either side, but to place it on your drinking side means the person seeing you drink is denied the pleasure of the decoration. A similar principle would apply to jugs.

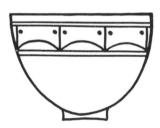 

If decorating a bowl it is pleasant to see a design as you look into the centre or a band design near the rim, either in or outside, or both, depending on the shape of the bowl. A wide bowl is best decorated inside while a closed shape will be enhanced by an outside decoration near the rim.

Circular lines are an easy decorating method, best done on a potters' wheel or turntable. Let the lines have an interesting rhythm. They are best executed with a fine-pointed Japanese brush. The brush is held very steady and wheel allowed to do the work.

There are many shapes to the *lidded pot*. It is best to have the decoration as a focal point, but not to be too overpowering and busy. There must be harmony between the object and the chosen design. Using the container for food should also be taken into consideration and heavy incisive lines avoided to prevent food particles from lodging in crevices.

Vases look well with well chosen brush designs or well-placed motifs, to give a pleasing result.

Decorating and embellishing a surface with line and colour is probably one of the earliest creative gestures of man.

Glossary of Terms

BISCUIT : Unglazed fired ware

BODY : the clay of which the pot is made

BRUSHES : the best brushes made for painting pottery are Japanese or Chinese.

CLAY SLIP : A clay in liquid suspension (creamy consistency).

GLAZE : A liquid suspension of finely ground minerals — applied by pouring, dipping or spraying onto a bisqued fired ware.

GLAZE FIRING : A firing cycle to the temperature at which the glaze materials will melt to form a glass-like surface.

GLOST FIRING : glaze firing

LEATHERHARD : Clay that can be moved slightly under pressure — compare hardness of leather.

OXIDATION : Electric kiln: an electric kiln always gives an oxidising fire. Gas, wood, oil or kerosine heated kiln: the firing of a kiln in such a manner that combustion is complete and in consequence the burning gases are supplied with oxygen, which causes metals in the clay and glaze to give their oxide colours.

REDUCTION : Normally done in a gas, oil, wood or kerosine kiln: a firing using insufficient oxygen, the carbon monoxide thus formed unites with oxygen from the body and glaze to form carbon dioxide producing colour changes in colouring oxides.

SGRAFFITO : Incising through a layer of slip or glaze or just cutting a design into the leather hard clay which must be thick enough to take this treatment.

TERRA COTTA : An earthernware body generally red in colour.

Wheelthrown terracotta pot with light clay slip band decoration in iron oxide

BANDS

These designs are suitable for cups, bowls, vases and slabwork. Suggested methods (see pages 6 & 7), could be Tooling, and then Burnishing or Inlay—Wax Resist, Raised Designs or Brush Painting.

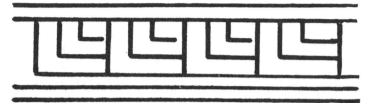
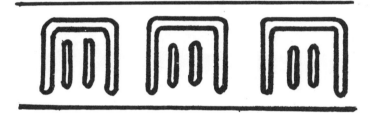
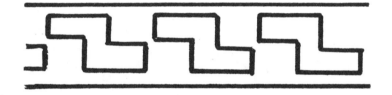
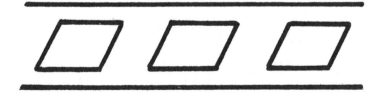
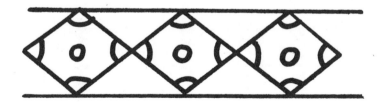

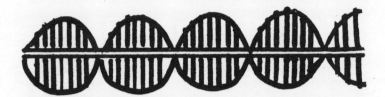

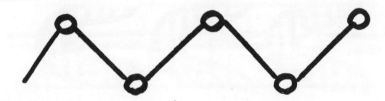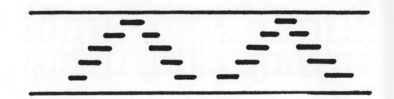
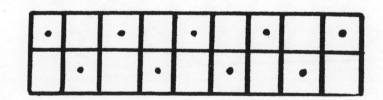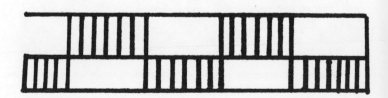

16

The bowl has been painted with manganese oxide before bisque firing. Clear, opaque or matt glaze is suitable. Glaze could be coloured — but if too dark will not allow the design to shine through.

CIRCLES

These designs, single or repeated, are suitable for bowls, plates, lidded boxes or vases.
Suggested decorating methods (see page 6) could be:
Tooling (lino tools or modelling tools) and then Inlay, Sgraffito, Wax Resist, Raised Design or Brush Painting.

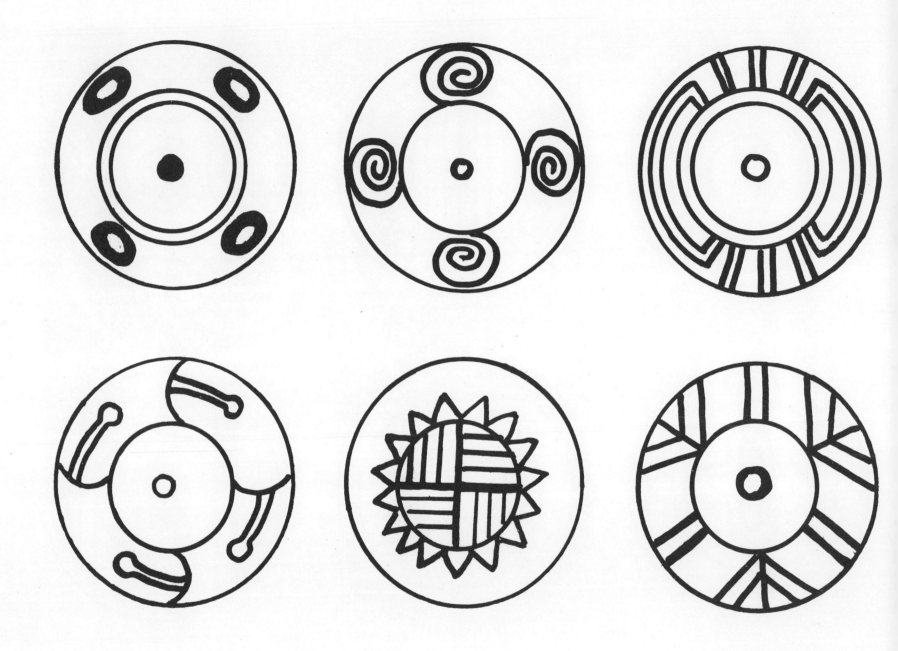

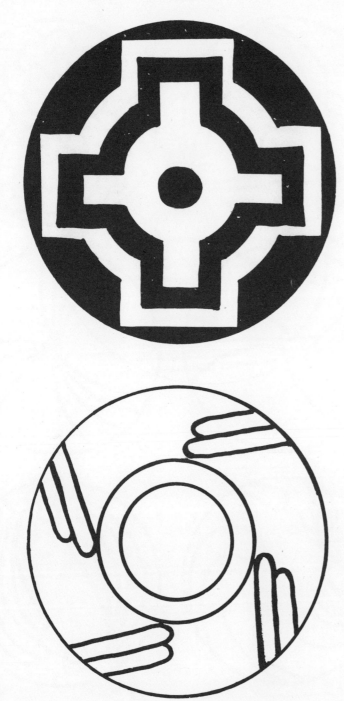
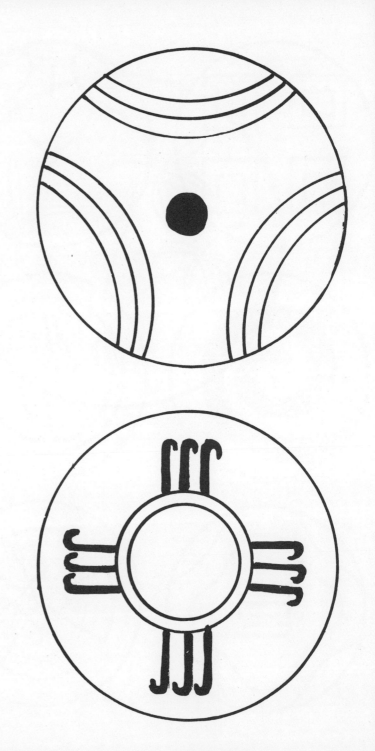

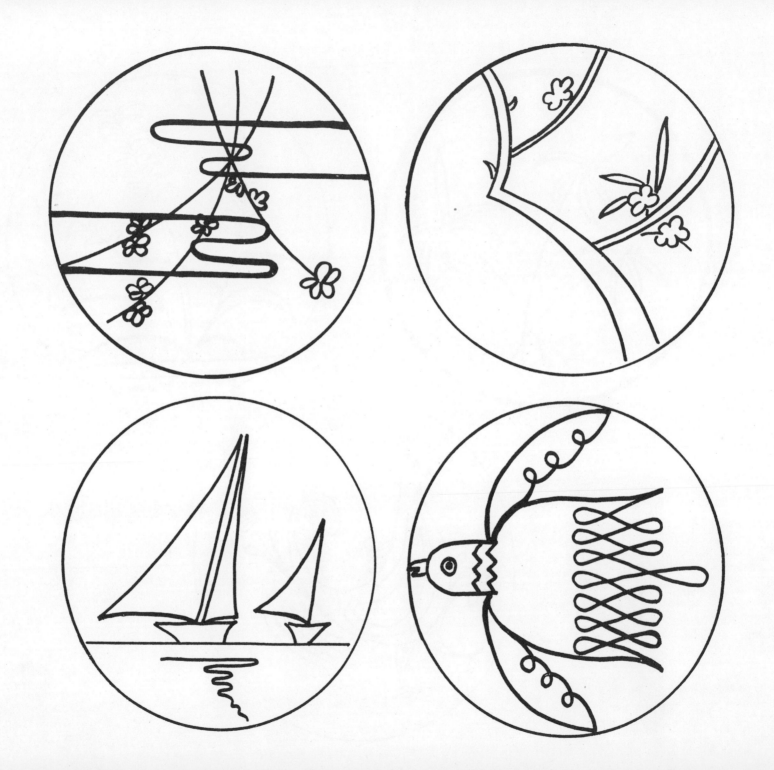

Handbuilt square vase with clay design added to front of pot. Background rubbed with manganese oxide.

SQUARES

These designs can be used on shallow dishes, tiles, square flower pots or on top of square boxes.
Suggested decorative methods (see pages 6 & 7) could be:
Tooling (lino tools or modelling tools) and then Inlay, and also Slip—Sgraffito, Wax Resist, Raised Design, Brush Painting.

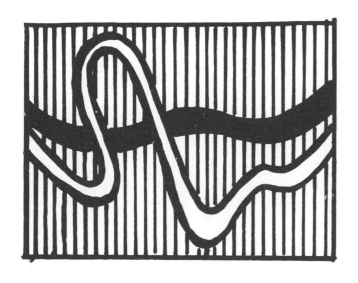

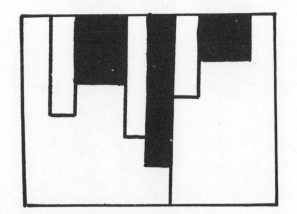

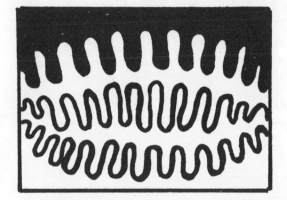
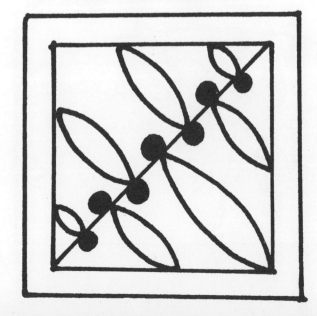

Handbuilt and wheelthrown, design of snake inlayed with darker clay, glazed in celedon and fired to stoneware.

ANIMALS

These designs can be used on bowls (inside or outside), on plates, cylinders, vases or cups. Suggested decorative method (see pages 6 & 7) could be:
Tooling (lino or modelling tools) and then Inlay, and also Sgraffito, Raised Design, Brush Painting or Sliptrailing.

The plate had black slip poured into the centre. The white and red design was syringed onto the black slip in a free form movement. The plate had to be leatherhard for this decoration. Clear, opaque or matt glazes are suitable, as long as the glaze does not obscure the design.

FREE FORM

These designs are suitable for cups, bowls, plates, slab dishes and vases.
Suggested decorative methods (see pages 6 & 7) could be:
Tooling (lino tools or modelling tools) and then Inlay, Sgraffito, Wax Resist, Raised Design, Brush Painting or Sliptrailing.

Plate had white slip poured over—three syringes filled with blue-chrome green and iron red slip formed the circles on a rotating wheel head. A knife point dragged the liquid slip into star pattern. Dots had the slip extended sideways with the point of the knife.

SLIPTRAILING

This method is suitable for platters—shallow bowls and tiles. See details on page 9.

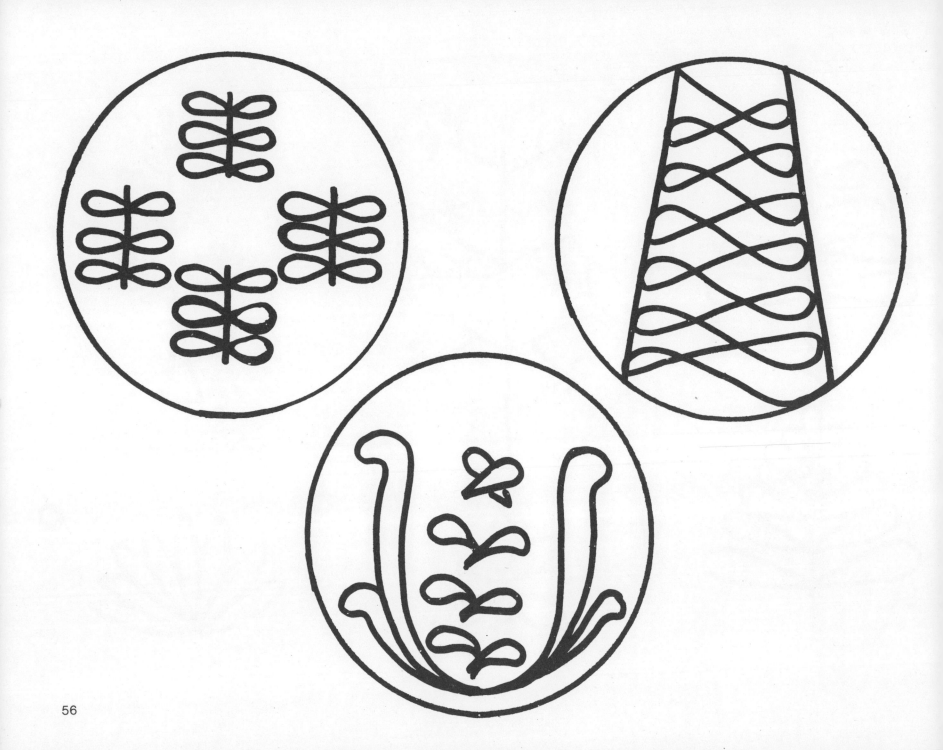

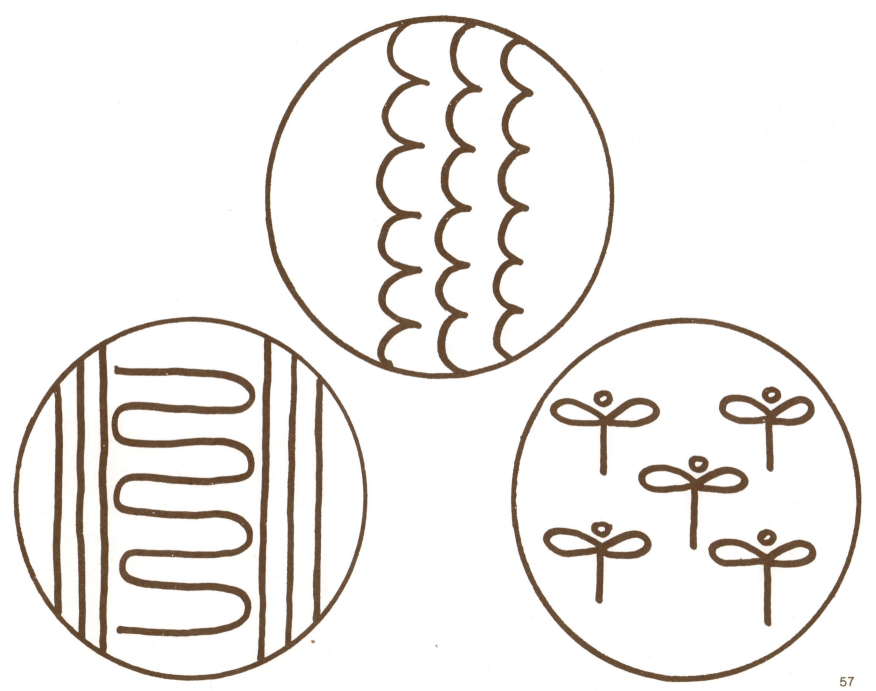

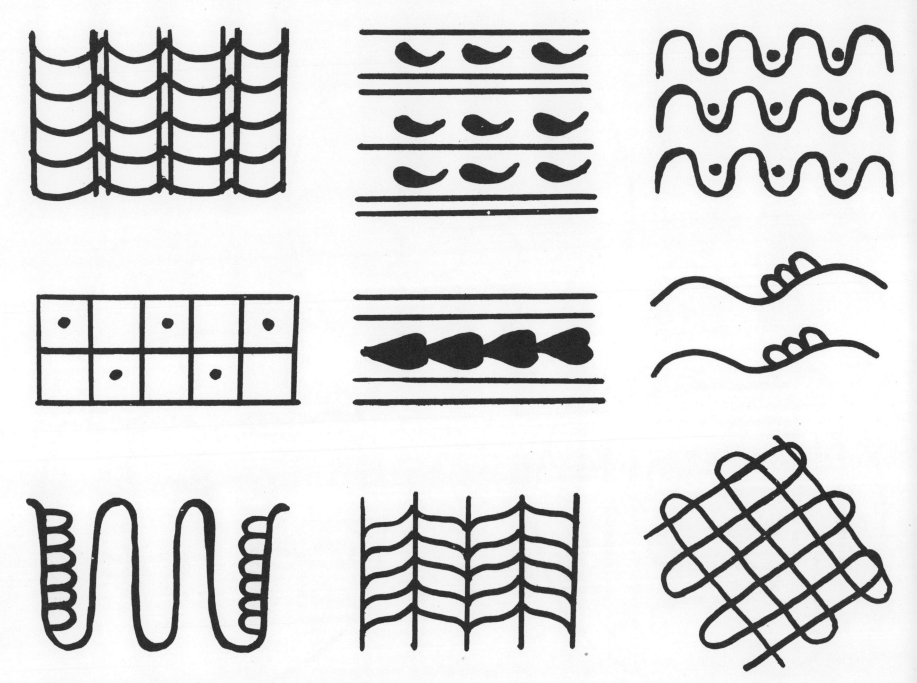

Bottle was glazed in an opaque stoneware glaze blue pigment mix painted on after glazing.

JAPANESE BRUSH PAINTING

These designs are suitable for plates, bowls, vases, cups and cylinders. A fine pointed brush is required for these Brush Paintings. Any oxide mixed with water, or suggested blue pigment (see page 8) can be used on either pre-bisqued or after-bisqued claybody —and also after glaze application.
It is important for the beginner to practise the strokes. Purchase of a book on Sumi-e is advisable in order to become familiar with the method of painting in this style.

64